Nouns, Verbs
and
Other Words
A Poetry Collection

Tawanda Prince

Rosie Lane
PUBLISHING

All definitions are taken from *http://dictionary.reference.com*

Printed in the United States of America
19 18 17 16 15   987654321

Published by Rosie Lane Publishing
For information contact Rosie Lane Publishing at
Rosielanepublishing@gmail.com
Author's website: ***www.Thegoodlifecoach.net***

ISBN: 978-0-692-45571-5

Book design: Tawanda Prince
Cover design: Kendall King- ***kkproductions.biz***
Front cover photograph: Tawanda Prince
Back cover photograph: Javon Prince
Editor: Wendy Stevens

Nouns, Verbs and Other Words

Nouns, Verbs and Other Words

Nouns, Verbs and Other Words

Dedication

This book is dedicated to those who have caused me
To think
To feel
To know
To grow
To flow

Nouns, Verbs and Other Words

Acknowledgements

Glory to God, the creator of all things beautiful! Thank you for choosing me to be an extension and expression of your divine masterworks. Also, thank you for gifting me with creative vision, uniqueness, boldness, courage and an open heart to share my words with the world.

To my parents who always encourage, support and believe in me...your continuous love is the wind beneath my wings.

To my children who are the offspring of love, purpose and creativity...I am so proud as I watch you both use your God-given gifts, talents and resources to pursue the great possibilities of THE GOOD LIFE.

Thanks Javon for having a good "eye" and capturing the back cover photo.

To my friends of distinction that comprise my creative circle...I love you and thank you for accepting me and allowing me to be me.

To my editor Wendy who serves with a heart of gold and a mean red pen...thanks for the edits, edits and more edits.

To my graphic artist Kendall...I said I wanted it in red...no blue...maybe orange...turquoise...ok red it is!

To the readers and thinkers...thank you for your eyes to see, ears to hear and hearts to believe.

Nouns, Verbs and Other Words

Nouns, Verbs and Other Words

Table of Contents

Nouns, Verbs and Other Words

Fore-WORD

Dr. Seuss first ignited my love for words, rhythm, rhyme and verse with cats, hats and things that match. Then Robert Frost ushered me beyond the walls of my fourth grade classroom into the very essence of the meaning of poetry. By fifth grade, when my friend Sharon shared her poetry with me, I was inspired and I dared to write.

My first poem, "Love is a Very Funny Game" *(yes I wrote about love in the fifth grade),* launched me into the creative vortex of nouns, verbs and other words. I was empowered to command the spaces between the lines, commas and all manner of punctuation. I was overwhelmingly compelled to speak my piece, have my say and tell my side, with rhythm and rhyme.

For years I was a closet poet, afraid to reveal my skills. However, finding the courage to bear my soul, expose my heart and divulge my dreams and secrets has been worth the risk. It is truly divine to connect with the souls of others. My words allow me to touch people and heal those broken places and release those who are bound.

Nouns, Verbs and Other Words, is the gathering of words about words, life, God, her, him, love and heartache. This collection of poems, written over a twenty year span, is the bridge to the heart, mind and soul of all who agree to listen and walk with me for just a little while…

Words about Words

WORD *(noun)*

A unit of language, consisting of one or more spoken sounds or their written representation that functions as a principal carrier of meaning; an expression or utterance.

Nouns, Verbs and Other Words

My Flow

My rhymes are very simple you see
But that doesn't mean it's not poetry
I may not spit like the young bucks today
I just simply say what I gotta say
My words are not sharp
My speech is not hard
I may speak about love
Or give praise to God
I may even rhyme at times like Dr. Seuss
Ah but my words can still be put to good use
And yes I ...in my mind...sometimes... I criticize
How my words may fall
But true poets know
That poetry cannot be
One size fits all

Nouns, Verbs and Other Words

My Inspiration

You inspire me to
Poetry

And poetry makes me
Feel free

And freedom is where
I want to be

Freedom to do with you
What I please

And pleasing you makes me
Feel free

And in freeing me
I find peace

In the midst of peace
I find love

In the midst of love
 I find you

And you inspire me to
Poetry

Nouns, Verbs and Other Words

Words about Life

LIFE *(noun)*

The general or universal condition of human existence: the animate existence or period of animate existence of an individual.

The Struggle is Real

We struggle in a world that doesn't accept us
We struggle to make our marks on jobs where they just suspect us
We struggle in relationships with partners who neglect us
We struggle within families where kinfolk reject us
We struggle to live in neighborhoods where the neighbors don't respect us
We struggle to escape the history that connects us
We struggle to speak a language that doesn't reflect us
We struggle to be heard in a nation where they don't want elect us
We struggle to be led by leaders who misdirect us
We struggle in a system where the laws don't protect us
We struggle to be loved by lovers who infect us
We struggle to be cured by doctors who just inject us
But we struggle toward the end
When God will resurrect us

Nouns, Verbs and Other Words

I'm Tired

I'm tired and my feet hurt
From climbing up the corporate ladder
And climbing up the rough side of the mountain
From kicking butt to protect what's mine
From tip-toeing on egg shells around his fragile feelings
From stomping out prejudice against my gender and my race
From always skating on thin ice
From marching to Zion in a one-woman band
From jumping through hoops
From trying to stay a step ahead
I'm tired and my feet hurt

I'm tired and my knees hurt
From kneeling to pray away my problems
From bending the rules
From sitting on the sideline
From rocking my babies on my lap
From scrubbing floors, toilets and baseboards
From tumbling over obstacles
From crouching in the corner with my pain
I'm tired and my knees hurt

I'm tired and my back hurts
From bending over backwards
From carrying the weight on my shoulders
From bowing and scraping just to get ahead
From having my back up against the wall
From backing away from unworthy suitors
From backing up my words with actions
From being stabbed in the back by so called friends
From holding back the love I want to give

Nouns, Verbs and Other Words

From holding back the tears from all the years
I'm tired and my back hurts

I'm tired and my head hurts
From thinking outside the box
From sorting through lies, misunderstandings and untruths
From heading in the wrong direction
From falling head over heels...again
From looking over my shoulder
From changing my focus from what was to what is
From balancing my walk with my talk
From imagining things that are not as though they were
From I think I can, I think I can, I think I can
I'm tired and my head hurts

Nouns, Verbs and Other Words

Rocking my Baby

I sit and rock my child to sleep
As I long for a strong hand
On the small of my back
To ease the weariness of the day

I embrace my child
While holding on to promises unmet
Clinging to dreams deferred
Longing for love unrequited

I stroke my child's hair
With hands that have stroked rejection
Carefully molded and embraced emptiness
And fanned the flames of disappointment

I rock my child to sleep
While shaking off curses from past generations
Loosening the dust of desperation
Lifting praises above circumstances

While rocking my child to sleep
I whisper prayers of overcoming
Chant verses of victory
Make proclamations of triumph

I rock my child to sleep
As I long for the love of the one
Who refused to place his hands on the small of my back
To ease the weariness of the day

Leave No Child Behind

Leave no child behind
That he may find
A place where he can discover
Who he was intended to be
Before the world was made
It is not too late
To save each boy and each girl
From a world waiting to swallow their dreams

Leave no child behind
That she may find
The treasures that live
Down on the inside
Where hope springs eternal
Reaching higher
And digging deeper
So roots can blossom

Leave no child behind
That he may find
A chance and a choice
To have his voice
Resound through generations
Each one reaching one
Teaching one, beseeching one
Who will make a difference

Leave no child behind
That she may find
That one plus one still equals two
And there is nothing she can't do
When given the road map to success

Nouns, Verbs and Other Words

Paved with opportunities
So she can be
What she wants to be

Leave no child behind
That they may find
There is a place in this world
For each boy and each girl

Let the Good Times Roll

Remember the times in days gone by
When we grooved to the sounds of The Jackson Five
Bell bottoms, peace signs and afro hairdos
Freedom was the thing that we fought to pursue
Gladys Knight, The Four Tops and The Temptations
This was a time of living with no limitations
Mood rings, afro picks and a little "bamboo"
Strobe lights, incense and platform shoes
Roller skates, mini-skirts and thigh-high boots
Everybody was busy searching for the truth
But Malcolm, Martin and Medgar died for the cause
Marches and meetings helped to open the doors
Soul train lines, picket signs and riots rang out loud
James Brown taught us to be black and proud
Richard Pryor, Dolomite and Redd Foxx made us smile
Chia pets, bean-bag chairs and phones we had to dial

Then the 80's rolled in with changes in our world
Some wore pink hair while some wore jheri curls
Boy George, Milli Vanilli and Michael was the "Thriller"
Inside and outside of the closet AIDS became a killer
Solid Gold, HBO, Showtime and MTV
Oprah and Arsenio proved that talk ain't cheap
The Cosby Show, A Different World, Prince and Morris Day
"Just Say No" and condoms became the only way

The 90's was a time of change with the 70's all grown up
Bill played the sax, had no sex and didn't inhale the "stuff"
Sister Act, Disappearing Acts, and Ghost was on the screen
Biggie Smalls and Tupac Shakur just up and left the scene
Michal Jackson said he did not touch and Magic had HIV
We wore acrylic nails, colored eyes, braids, wigs and weaves
Mike Tyson and O.J. Simpson made headlines more than twice
Jessie Jackson had a little secret that wasn't very nice

Nouns, Verbs and Other Words

The new millennium in the land of the "Bush" and the pain of 911
Condoleezza and Collin Powell like the Jeffersons had moved on up
Halle Berry and Denzel Washington made Hollywood history
The Grammys showed Alicia Keys battle India Arie
Ellen came out, Allyiah flew home and the Columbia blew up
Venus and Serena took home the championship cup
Now the world has changed and changed again with lots of evidence
The United States of America has a black man President
But marches, meetings and riots still ring out loud
There's Obamacare, iPads, iPods and gays can marry now
Freddie's dead, Trayvon is gone and we can't forget Mike Brown
Unemployment is up, communities down and homelessness abounds
American Idol, Empire, Catfish and Orange is the New Black
Drones flew beyond the White House wall perhaps to plan attack
Whitney's gone, "Housewives" are hot and Scandal is all the rage
And everyone reveals their lives on their Facebook page
All in all it has been quite a ride that is something to behold
From here and now, time marches on so let the good times roll

Nouns, Verbs and Other Words

Words about God

GOD *(noun)*

The one Supreme Being, the creator and ruler of the universe.

Sacred

Water is sacred
Wood, sand and trees are sacred
Lightening, rocks and leaves are sacred
Wind is sacred
Snow is sacred
The way the river flows is sacred
The stars and planets in the sky are sacred
The Light, the Light, the Light is sacred

Fire is sacred
Ice is sacred
The origin of everything nice is sacred
Love is sacred
A deer is sacred
Music to my ear is sacred
My soul is sacred
My hole is sacred
And mysteries that unfold are sacred
Freedom is sacred
Peace is sacred
And every part of me is sacred

Sacred is as sacred does
It's what's to come and what once was
My heart beat is sacred
My breath is sacred
Every single footstep is sacred
My soul is sacred
My spirit is sacred
The God who lives in me is sacred
Prayer is sacred
Song is sacred

Nouns, Verbs and Other Words

Tears that babies cry are sacred
Space is sacred
The rain is sacred
And even sometimes my pain is sacred

My flow is sacred
My vibe is sacred
My rhythm and my rhyme are sacred
My joy is sacred
The blood is sacred
The power of God's love is sacred
Sacred is the sun that shines
And sacred berries still make wine
A bee is sacred
A bird is sacred
Nouns, verbs and words are sacred

Nouns, Verbs and Other Words

Strange Fruit

Like strange fruit
He hung on a tree
He died to save you and me
His cleansing blood
Redemption gave
Now I'm saved, I'm saved

Like strange fruit
He stayed on the tree
He wouldn't come down
Just so I could be free
His cleansing blood
Healing gave
Now I'm saved, I'm saved

Like strange fruit
He bore the disdain of the tree
He hung in shame
Because I am so guilty
His cleansing blood
Freedom gave
Now I'm saved, I'm saved

Like strange fruit
He groaned upon a tree
He bled and died
And suffered silently
His cleansing blood
Purpose gave
Now I'm saved, I'm saved

Nouns, Verbs and Other Words

Like strange fruit
They cut him down from the tree
He went in the tomb
But rose up in three
His cleansing blood
Eternity gave
Thank God I'm saved, I'm saved

A Miracle

God gave us a miracle
He sent it yesterday
He revealed his healing power
In the most miraculous way
His hands repaired the body
His love repaired the heart
He proved when things seem impossible
A miracle he will impart

God gave us a miracle
To him all thanks be given
He proved that he is Lord of all
Master of earth and heaven
And with this precious miracle
He gave us even more
A chance to love and serve him
More fully than before

Yes, God gave us a miracle
Right before our very eyes
He answered our humble prayers
And dried our sorrowful cries
If there is no other miracle
That we will ever know
He gave us eternal life
Because he loves us so

Nouns, Verbs and Other Words

Words about Her

HER *(pronoun)*

Refers to a female person or animal being discussed or previously mentioned.

Nouns, Verbs and Other Words

My Sister's Keeper

When she is hungry, I feed her
When she is naked, I clothe her
When she is cold, I warm her
When she is hot, I cool her
Am I my sister's keeper?

When she is broken, I mend her
When she is sick, I heal her
When she is crying, I hold her
When she is dying, I revive her
Am I my sister's keeper?

When she is lonely, I comfort her
When she is angry, I calm her
When she is confused, I guide her
When she is misused, I protect her
Am I my sister's keeper?

When she is barren, I birth for her
When she is abandoned, I receive her
When she is burdened, I relieve her
When she is trying, I believe in her
Am I my sister's keeper?

I am my sister's keeper
A charge I can't deny
Her load I bear because I know
In time she'll carry mine
Yes, I am my sister's keeper
Connected through the heart
Every woman is my sister
And nothing can keep us apart
I am my sister's keeper

Nouns, Verbs and Other Words

Pour Into Me Oh God

Pour into me oh God
Let your spirit fill me
Pour into me oh God
Let your peace enthrall me
Let your love seep into every broken place
Pour into me oh God
Fill me with your light
Consume me with your warmth
Illuminate my heart
That I may see myself
From your view

Pour into me oh God
May the lessons of the past
Guide and direct my path
Order my steps with the gift of knowing
Pour into me oh God
Fill me with your truth
Pour into me oh God
Fill me with your message
That I may tell a dying world
Of your saving grace and mercy
Pour into me oh God
That I may be a reflection of you

Nouns, Verbs and Other Words

Single Christian

When you see a single Christian
Some things you shouldn't say
Like "Oh, it's not so bad girl"
Or "You'll get married someday"

They don't really need your pity
They don't really need your blame
"You're better off without him"
Is what you shouldn't say

Single is not a sickness
It's not the "lonely disease"
Don't tell her she's a great catch
Or "Girl, I wish that it was me"

Singles don't need to be reminded
That this is the best time of life
She doesn't need to be reminded
That she will make the perfect wife

"Just hold on love is coming"
Is not the thing to say
Don't tell her Jesus is her boyfriend
And all she should do is pray

Yes single is a season
Not a condition to regret
It's the time of preparation
For the heart she hasn't met

Next time you see a single Christian
This one thing you can say
God has a plan for every life
Just continue to follow His way

Nouns, Verbs and Other Words

While I Wait...

Lord be with me...while I wait
Help me to be faithful to you...while I wait
Ease the pain...while I wait
Apply your salve of love to my broken pieces...while I wait
Make me ready...while I wait
Catch my tears in a jar...while I wait
Hold my dreams in a bottle...while I wait
Hold back the night...while I wait
Love me, love me, just love me Lord...while I wait
Help me to love myself...while I wait
Help me to please you Lord...while I wait
Transform me...while I wait
Teach me to resist temptation...while I wait
Lord give me peace...while I wait
Lord help me dream...while I wait
Lord dry my tears...while I wait
Lord calm my fears...while I wait
Cool my fire but not my flame...while I wait
Give me vision...while I wait
Give me provision...while I wait
Release the toxins...while I wait
Carry the burdens...while I wait
Lord help me to believe...while I wait

Nouns, Verbs and Other Words

Words about Him

HIM *(pronoun)*

Refers to a male person or animal being discussed or previously mentioned.

Nouns, Verbs and Other Words

The Making of a True Warrior

The heart of a true warrior
Is tender yet tough
He beseeches God for guidance and strength
And leans not to his own understanding
With courage he walks boldly into the fire
And he is not defeated by the fiery darts of the adversary

The essence of a true warrior
Is mighty yet meek
He is a conqueror and an overcomer
Though he may slay giants
And climb mountains
He never considers himself more highly than he ought

The spirit of a true warrior
Is resilient yet resigned
To accept his God appointed and anointed assignment
Always restless and ready
To bounce back from any setbacks
Turning stumbling blocks into stepping stones

The valor of a true warrior
Is always seeking to protect and defend the weak
Even if it costs him his own dreams
He is ready for battle
As he keeps watch at the gate
Wearing the full armor of God

The soul of a true warrior
Is playful yet cautious
As he carefully orchestrates the dance
Between offensive and defensive maneuvers

34

Nouns, Verbs and Other Words

He enjoys wielding the sword of the spirit
And lashes offenders with his tongue

A true warrior
Is armed and extremely dangerous
He is always positioned for battle
Courageous in struggle and victorious in warfare
Knowing that he can do all things through Christ who
strengthens him
Are you a true warrior?

Watching You, Watching Me

He doesn't know that I see him watching me
His eyes drink me in
And his lips smile with approval
He chases me through
The fantasies in his mind
And he watches to see
If I will let him catch me
His hands reach out to touch places
That are hidden from plain view

He caresses my dreams
And I dream of him
His gaze goes deep
Even into the soul
Where my desires
Are carefully tucked away and
Hidden from plain view
He doesn't know that
I see him watching me
As I flirt with possibilities
Of visions unexplored
He doesn't know that
I watch him too

Nouns, Verbs and Other Words

Southern Comfort

Let me slip inside your southern comfort
And warm myself in the glow of your smile
As I indulge myself in your southern comfort
Let me kick off my shoes
And run barefoot through your heart
A heart that is as warm as the sun
As I wrap myself inside
Your southern comfort
I lose myself as we become one heartbeat
And you are so easy to love
So easy to love

Where I belong is nestled deep inside
The crevices of your southern comfort
With starry nights and moonlit kisses
Where one minute lasts forever
Where promises like trees sway in the breeze
And sizzle from the heat of the fire
That burns with an eternal flame
Such a perfect fit inside your southern comfort
My heart found its way home
You are so easy to love; so easy to love

Nouns, Verbs and Other Words

Words about Love

LOVE *(noun)*

A profoundly tender, passionate affection for another person; a feeling of warm personal attachment or deep affection; sexual passion or desire.

LOVE *(verb)*

To have a strong liking for; take great pleasure in; to embrace and kiss (someone), as a lover; to have sexual intercourse with someone.

Hello

It's amazing how life can change in an instant
With just the sound of one hello
Echoing in the darkness of the night
A chance meeting...perhaps
Or maybe just fate and destiny

And love blew in with a whisper
That lingered from lifetimes gone by
And memories yet to come
And it was as if hello meant I found you
And the wait is finally over

Two spirits so familiar, yet strangers unknown
At the open door of love divine
And time stood still, so still
At the dawn of what was meant to be
A dream fulfilled by a love
That transcends comprehension and dimensions
Yes, so amazing how life can change in an instant
With just the sound of one hello
And I don't mind...

My Soul

My soul searched for you
Destination unknown
Looking but never finding
The missing piece to my puzzle

My soul longed for you
To be held in arms unknown
To be wrapped up in you
And finding myself complete

My soul ached for you
Needing love to replace pain
And together to replace lonely
And me to become we

My soul waited for you
Believing that someday
You would come to find me
And my heart would be yours

My soul searched for you
Waiting for you to appear
Out of the darkness
Your soul found a home

Nouns, Verbs and Other Words

I-N-T-I-M-A-C-Y

I-N-T-I-M-A-C-Y
Into-me-see
See my heart
See my love
See my peace
See my pain
See my strength
See my passion
See my bliss
See my longing
See my kiss
See my secrets
See my dreams
See my pleasure
See my treasure
See my truth
See my wishes
See my joy
See my beauty
I-N-T-I-M-A-C-Y
Into-me-see
And love me

Nouns, Verbs and Other Words

More...

More than forever
More than just enough
More than I love you
More than just a touch

More than a promise
More than a glance
More than a feeling
More than the "dance"

More than...more than
More than a song
More than your kisses
More than to belong

More than I need you
More than I breathe
More than you are giving
More than I receive

More than tomorrow
More than today
More than what is to come
More than what you say

More, more, more
You always leave me wanting more...

Nouns, Verbs and Other Words

Words about Heartache

Heartache *(noun)*

Emotional pain or distress; sorrow; grief; anguish.

The Game

Strike one!
How did this happen again
I messed around and fell in love with him
At first it was a game
And I played the game well
But my heart got involved
And that's when I fell
He was quite a catch
So I chased him to play
But love was no match
And my heart got in the way
I didn't expect him to just knock me off my feet
I didn't know he would give love so sweet

Strike two!
How did this happen again
I played around and now I can't win
The ball is in my court
And I don't want to let him go
Can I play for keeps; I really don't know
I played with him and he played me back
Was it a fair game
Or was the deck stacked?

Foul ball!
I really messed up this time
I never saw it coming
They say love is blind
The one-two punch caught me by surprise
If the winner takes all, which one takes the prize?

Nouns, Verbs and Other Words

Touch Down!
I wasn't prepared, I let my guard down
I didn't know that love would wrestle me to the ground
I didn't protect myself
My heart was open wide
He made a quick move and I let him inside
Now the game is not fun
There is too much at stake
Will it be check?
Or is it check mate?

Nouns, Verbs and Other Words

You Never Bought Me Diamonds

You never bought me diamonds
Nor rubies or pearls
Never called me precious
Nor said I was your girl
You never held my hand
To stroll down lover's lane
Never worked to make things better
Never tried to ease my pain

You never bought me diamonds
Nor springtime flowers in bloom
Never called me your honey
Nor asked me to jump the broom
You don't know my favorite color
Nor my favorite kind of tea
You don't know when I started school
Nor finished my degree

You never bought me diamonds
Nor chocolates for me to munch
You never took me to a movie
Or even out to lunch
I have never met your family
And you have not met mine
I don't know the friends you keep
Nor where you spend your time

You never bought me diamonds
Nor wrote poems with my name
You never asked what I was feeling
You just simply ran your game
But one day I'll get diamonds
Some flowers, chocolates and all
But for now I'll have to face the fact
It was just a booty call

Nouns, Verbs and Other Words

Haunted House

Ghosts and goblins
Monsters and ghouls
My house is haunted
Cause I've been a fool
Skeletons in my closet
Bones on my floor
Remnants and fragments
Of a life that is no more

Black cat in the window
Witches brew in the pot
Spooks in the alley
Trying to get what I got
And I gave of myself
When the fire got hot

Jack was no lantern
And the monster didn't mash
The noise that was heard
Was my heart as it crashed
When the mummy came walking
With his crystal balls
My house wasn't ready
Cob webs on my walls
He slipped in beside me
And troubled my head
My house became haunted
When he got in my bed

Nouns, Verbs and Other Words

Rats and rattlesnakes
Spiders and worms
Taunting and teasing
Each one took a turn
This vampire was thirsty
For a taste of my blood
Each kiss was more deadly
Each time we made love

Then he just vanished
Before one early dawn
Blood on my carpet
Tombstone on my lawn
Now my house is haunted
There is no doubt
I can't escape it
My secret is out
Skeletons in my closet
Bones on my floor
Remnants and fragments
Of a life that is no more.

Nouns, Verbs and Other Words

No More

No more crumbs on my table
No more socks on my floor
No more lover who ain't able
No more, no more, no more

No more, "Baby I'm sorry"
No more listening at the door
No more need to sit and worry
No more, no more, no more

No more phone numbers in your pocket
No more hang ups on my phone
No more picture in my locket
No more, no more, no more

No more bills I didn't make
No more keeping score
No more kisses that are fake
No more, no more, no more

No more lies and misunderstandings
No more, "Baby I can't recall"
No more ego that's expanding
No more, no more, no more

No more touches at midnight
No more making love on the floor
No more feeling that feels so right
No more, no more, no more

No more dreams about tomorrow
No more yearning at my core
No more heart that's filled with sorrow
No more, no more, no more

Nouns, Verbs and Other Words

Nouns, Verbs and Other Words

www.ingramcontent.com/pod-product-compliance
Lightning Source LLC
Chambersburg PA
CBHW061756040426

42447CB00011B/2324